Family World

My Brother

Caryn Jenner

FRANKLIN WATTS
LONDON•SYDNEY

Sharing this book

This book shows the relationships of brothers with their siblings in children's lives around the world. It provides a useful starting point to discuss how families everywhere are similar, but that each child's family is different and special.

• Remember that families are formed in different ways and a brother can be a step-brother, half-brother, adoptive brother, foster brother or any boy that a child thinks of as a brother.
• Family life is rewarding, but sometimes it can also be difficult.
Ask your GP, health visitor or school for advice.

These organisations also offer help to families:
Family Lives – www.familylives.org.uk; Parentline 0808 800 2222
Family Links – www.familylinks.org.uk
Gingerbread (especially for single-parent families) – www.gingerbread.org.uk

First published in 2013 by Franklin Watts
Copyright © Franklin Watts 2013

Franklin Watts
338 Euston Road
London NW1 3BH

Franklin Watts Australia
Level 17/207 Kent Street
Sydney, NSW 2000

All rights reserved.

Series Editor: Sarah Peutrill
Series Designer: Ruth Walton

Dewey number 306.8'75
ISBN: 978 1 4451 1931 1
Printed in Malaysia

Franklin Watts is a division of Hachette Children's Books, an Hachette UK company. www.hachette.co.uk

Picture credits: AISPIX by Image Source/Shutterstock: 10c, 14c. Andresr/Shutterstock: 4c. Petur Asgeirsson/Shutterstock: 5b. Atlas pix/Shutterstock: 5cl, 6t. Syaheir Azizan/Shutterstock: 9b, 22c. Michael Blackburn/istockfoto: 23tl. Brocreative/Shutterstock: 6b. c/Shutterstock: 14br. Augusto Cabral/Shutterstock: 5tl, 6c, 12tl. Lucian Coman/Shutterstock: 8c. creatista/ istockfoto: 23bl. Distinctive Images/Shutterstock: 16b. EVA fotographic/istockfoto: 9tr. forestpath/Shutterstock: 13c. gabor2100/Shutterstock: 20-21. Globe Turner/Shutterstock: 12c,19tl. Mandy Godbehear/ Shutterstock: 12cl. Michael Jung/Shutterstock: 17c. Aleksey Klints/Shutterstock: 16tl. Pavel L. Photo/Shutterstock:18c. R J Lerich/Shutterstock: 6cl. Artem Loskutnikov/Shutterstock: 4cl. Dmitry Matrosov/Shutterstock: 11c. MaxPhoto/Shutterstock: back cover, 5c. Maxslu/Shutterstock: 15c. mojito.mak[dog]gmail[dot] com/Shutterstock: 13tl. Vikram Raghuvanshi/istockfoto: 23tlc, 23tr, 23cl, 23ccl, 23ccr, 23cr, 23br. Rhozhkovs/Shutterstock: 9cl. M Shep 2/istockfoto: 19c. Shutterstock: 10tr. Smile Studio/ Shutterstock: 8tl, 16c. Paul Stringer/Shutterstock: 9tc, 15tl, 18tl. Pal Teravagimov/Shutterstock: front cover. Frances Twitty/ istockfoto: 16cl. wikipedia: 7tr. Forest Woodward / istockfoto: 7c. Elena Yakusheva/Shutterstock: 12b. yellowcrestmedia/ istockfoto:lc. 23t Maric Zurov/Shutterstock: 11tl.

Please note: Some of the pictures in this book are posed by models. All scenarios are fictitious and any similarities to people, living or dead, are purely coincidental.

Contents

Brothers

Do you have a brother? Your brother is a boy with the same parents as you.

Ricardo and Diego live in Ecuador. They like being brothers. It means there's always someone to play with.

In South Africa, Ashanti and Teshi have a half-brother called Kwame. They all have the same mum, but Kwame has a different dad. The girls love their big brother!

Gloria's family is from Guatemala. Her brother, Pablo, thinks he looks grown up in his fake moustache!

Older and younger

You can have older brothers or younger brothers, or both! Twins or triplets are the same age.

Luis and his older brother, Geovany, live in Nicaragua. Sometimes Luis thinks his big brother is too serious, but other times he's lots of fun.

In Italy, Rosa's family has just adopted her little brother, Lorenzo, so now he is part of the family too.

Every day, Panyin and
her twin brother, Ochen,
race home from school
in Malawi.

Is your brother older or younger than you, or the same age?

Pals at play

Playing is what brothers do best!

Mandisa, Zarina and their brother, Oni, take turns to jump the rope in Botswana.

Gerta is from Switzerland. Her brother, Josef, has Down's Syndrome and some games are hard for him to learn. Gerta has made a special game that they play together.

Dara and her brother, Aran, play marbles in Malaysia.

?

What do you play with your brother?

Joking around

Brothers often tease and joke around because they think it's funny.

In Spain, Maria's dad is married to Hector's mum. Hector is Maria's step-brother. Sometimes Maria laughs at Hector's silly jokes and sometimes she just groans.

Jose is from Cuba. Most of the time, Jose doesn't mind when his big brothers tease him. He knows they love him.

Teasing and joking around is usually harmless, but not if it hurts someone's feelings.

We're a team

A brother can help you and make working together fun. It's good to have a brother on your team!

Rob and Ryan wash the family car in Canada. The car gets clean while the brothers get wet!

Zoe and her step-brother, Andrew, look after their new kitten in Australia.

In Thailand, Ratana and her brother, Niran, help each other on the computer. They make a good team.

?

How do you and your brother help each other? Do you make a good team?

Squabbles

Sometimes, brothers get angry and argue. (So do sisters!) The best thing to do is to calm down and sort out the problem.

In Britain, Caroline and her brother, Oliver, argue over a teddy bear. They would have a lot more fun if they shared the teddy instead.

Marco and Eduardo are brothers who live in Argentina. Right now they are angry with each other, but they'll feel much better when they start talking again.

?

Do you and your brother argue sometimes? Think how to sort out the problem instead of arguing.

Being kind

Brothers can be kind too.

Katya's family lives in Russia. Whenever Katya is frightened, she knows her twin brother, Aleksy, will comfort her.

Bashir and his little brother, Fahad, are from Indonesia. When Fahad gets tired, Bashir gives him a ride on his back.

In the United States, Bailey lets his brother, Shaun, take a turn with his new football.

?

What does your brother do that is kind? Do you do kind things for him?

Friends for life

A brother can be your friend
for your whole life.

Danika and her brother, Pavel, play in
their tent in Slovakia. Sometimes they
argue, but most of the time they like
being together.

Ada and her brother, Jomo, live in Liberia. Even when they are both grown up, Ada knows that they will still be special friends.

A world of families

Children just like you live all around the world. Some children *have* brothers and some children *are* brothers. Every child's family is different and special in its own way, but families everywhere also have many things in common.

Canada

Great Britain

Spain

United States

Nicaragua

Cuba

Guatemala

Ecuador

Liberia

Argentina

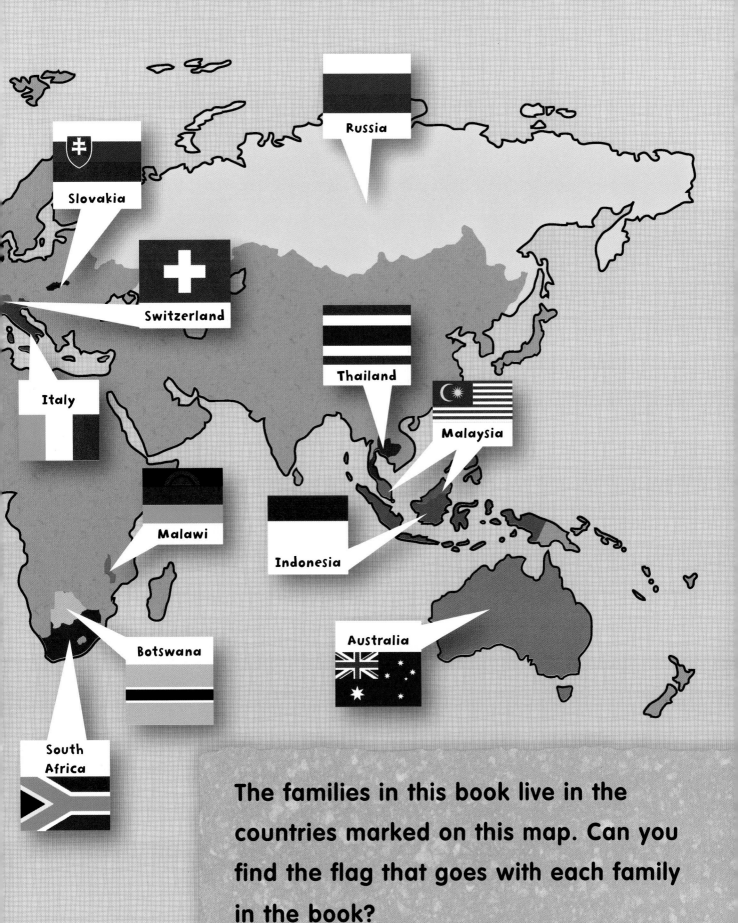

The families in this book live in the countries marked on this map. Can you find the flag that goes with each family in the book?

Activities

Make a star chart for you and your brother

See how well you can get along with your brother! Make a star chart to show how you are doing and give each other lots of stars for things like sharing and taking turns. Remember – if you make each other cross, then try and sort it out instead of arguing.

Find out how children around the world say 'brother'

Find out how to say brother in different languages. Ask friends who speak other languages, or look it up in books or on the Internet. Here are a few languages to get you started:

Swahili – Ndugu   Swedish – Bror
Italian – Fratello   Greek – Adelfos
Japanese – Ani (older brother); Ototo (younger brother)

Take turns choosing a game

First ask your brother what game he'd like to play. After you've played his game, then you choose a game to play. After a while, you'll make a habit of taking turns.

Make a family tree

A family tree shows the people in your family. Draw a picture of yourself and each person in your family, or use photos. On another sheet of paper, draw a tree. Stick your family pictures onto your tree. Your family tree can show the people you live with, or it can show lots of people in your family. You can even include your pets!

Granny and Grandad
(Mum's parents)

Grandma and Grandpa
(Dad's parents)

Mum

My uncle
(Mum's little brother)

My uncle
(Dad's big brother)

Dad

Me!

My brother

Words about families

Here are some words you may use when talking about families.

Adopted – becoming part of a family that is not the family you were born into

Divorced – when parents split up and are no longer married

Family – a group of people who love and care for each other and are usually related

Foster mum or dad – grown-ups who look after you in their family if your parents can't

Grandparents – your mum and dad's parents

Half-brother or half-sister – a brother or sister who has the same mum or dad as you, but the other parent is different

Parents – your mum and dad

Siblings – brothers and sisters

Step-brother or step-sister – the son or daughter of your step-mum or step-dad

Step-mum or step-dad – if your parents are divorced and one of them marries again, the new wife or husband would be your step-mum or step-dad

Index